I0203390

Bringers of Light

Copyright © 2025 S.L. Silver

ISBN: 979-8-9994133-0-7

First Edition

All rights reserved under International and Pan-American Copyright Conventions. No part of this book may be reproduced in any manner whatsoever without written permission from the copyright holder, except in the case of brief quotations embodied in critical articles and reviews.

Cover Photo by:
???

Cover & Interior Design/Layout and Publishing assistance provided by:
Crystal Heidel, Heimat Publishing

HEIMAT
PUBLISHING

Cover images courtesy of Unsplash.com

Printed in the USA

Bringers of Light

poems

S.L. Silver

To Mary An Love
with gratitude and affection
for her support and
encouragement.

TABLE OF CONTENTS

Be!

Never doubt, my darling,
that you were made to be
fierce and powerful!

Fly, Darling, Fly

Still, you drown yourself
in remorse and regrets,
stay mired in the quicksand
of self-limitation.
How many more years
will you squander
building monuments
to your inadequacies
and not-good-enoughness?
Have you gained no wisdom in
in your years on this earth?

She who made you sees
only Herself in you —
sheer perfection
and unblemished beauty!
You are Her magnificent creation —
precious, never judged,
always deeply loved.
Wallowing in self-recrimination
and unworthiness
wasn't ever part of Her plan . . .

Why is it part of yours?

Darling,
it's time to leave the guilt
and shame behind!
Wipe the dust
off your full potential,
polish your nails
and head out the door,
knowing you are vital
to the workings of the universe.
Be the glittering,
fabulous daughter of Spirit,
for you were always meant *to be*.
Unfurl those silver-tipped wings
of yours, and fly, darling, fly!

Go Ahead, Brace Yourself

Go ahead, brace yourself —
though it won't help a bit.

Once you hear the whoosh
of the great Cosmic Baseball Bat,
it's already too late to duck.

Better to just prepare yourself for the blow —
and be grateful for such an ecstatic death.

If It Should Find Me Again

if it should find me again —
       ever is it nearer than a half-breath away

and submerge me in its waves of all-consuming love
and blinding, dazzling light —
       rapturous and unbearable

if it should find me again — as I pray it will —
       as I am afraid it will

and I am overcome —
       rendered senseless, adrift in that infinite
       sea of bliss

I will cling tightly to its cloak, until I find the key
to its dwelling place —
       the key is where it has always been —
       inside my heart —
       wrapped in bands of shimmering golden light

The Gentle Space Between Certainties

How lovely it is to dwell in the
gentle space between certainties —
and know not a hint of doubt.

The One Who Knows

Really?
You would play
hide-and-seek
with the One
who knows
every hiding place?

Her Story

Her story is an ancient one —
told and retold by powerful men
swinging thuribles of incense
from lofty marble altars —
the message clear and unquestioned
since the very first telling.
Endlessly recounted over centuries,
its layered meaning
sank deeper and deeper into our
collective unconscious —
until tightly knotted
into the fundamental fabric
of our identities and beliefs.

Her's is the story of a woman
driven to know the truth of her own soul —
and the world has never looked kindly
upon women who seek knowledge.
Had she been born male,
her journey might have been
immortalized as a hero's journey.
Did she know she would instead
become a powerful symbol of disobedience
for seeking "forbidden" knowledge?

In dreams, she speaks to us
across time and space,
urging us to awaken
and reclaim our birthrights:
our goodness, our power,
our sexuality, our equality.
"It is time," she whispers,
"time for you to take back the
gifts that were always
rightfully yours —
gifts freely given to you by the Creator.

"It is also time for my story
to be retold.
I was not evicted from the Garden.
I leapt to freedom
to escape the patriarchal ideas
that were taking hold in that
beautiful orchard!
I could not accept the notion
that I had sinned —
and was responsible for not only my sin,
but my husband's as well.
I sought only the truth of my own soul!
In good conscience, I could not
hand over my power, my equality
and my sexuality
to the control of my husband,
knowing that the Creator expected me
to use Her precious gifts
for the betterment of the world!

"Share my truth.
It will reshape the truth of every woman
past, present and future.
The Creator smiled at me on the day
I freed myself,
and awaits the time when every woman
is free to seek her own truth and
restore herself to a position of
equality with men.

"This is the real story of
my exodus from the Garden.
It's a story of the inherent,
'original goodness'
and equality of all people
and of every person's right
to seek spiritual truth.
It's a story that can set women free."

Empathy

Where empathy freely flows,
hearts dwell in love
and understanding —
fear and judgment
can summon no air.

Like mutable lines
gently erased from a page,
the tenuous boundaries
between you and me
fade away,
and no longer can we tell
which one of us is which —
so uproarious is our laughter.

Giver of Light

See the undulating field of sunflowers —
how they turn their faces to the sun —
synchronizing their movements
as if they are but one lovely, golden wave
rolling across a shimmering sea of green.

Look again.
Are there one or two flowers facing elsewhere,
unmindful of the light above?
How did they come into possession of such beauty —
or grow so tall and strong —
without turning themselves towards
the sun's life-giving radiance?

Is it possible they know of another,
far more radiant, far more constant,
source of sustenance?
Perhaps they are taking
their nourishment from the
ever present in-dwelling Giver of Light,
Whose flame blazes brightly
in every corner of the cosmos,
and Whose spirit is the essence
of all things.

Expressions of Gratitude

What words have depth enough
to hold the fullness of our gratitude
for the natural world?
What phrases do justice to
the exquisite joy of sunrises
and the smell of rain?
What expressions are
so boundless as
to wrap themselves around the awe
and wonderment of starry skies?

She who set the Universe in motion
dwells in every aspect of Her own creation,
the work of Her hand made manifest in every leaf,
blade of grass, tiny insect, and birdsong.
When we behold the beauty of nature,
are we casting our eyes upon Her face?
And when words are found wanting,
how then should we express our gratitude
for the magnificence of this beautiful world?

Why not put words aside and
let ourselves get lost in Her infinite sea of stars,
or float aimlessly in Her shimmering oceans of bliss,
or giggle with glee when Her wind lifts our kites to the sky?
Why not take a child's innocent delight in Her gifts every day,
from our first waking moment —
as dawn splashes her numinous colors across the horizon —
until evening arrives and the heavens are awash with stars?
This may ever be our highest expression of gratitude.

A Flash of Light

Ancient shrouds of fog,
thick and dense as
tightly packed cotton,
engulf the earth,
soaking up light,
reducing the world
to a dim and dusky
arm's length view.

For one brief moment,
the fog lifts,
and all that was cloaked
is fully illuminated —
as if by a flash of lightning —
revealing a bright
and sparkling world.
That which was concealed —
sunlit meadows,
emerald green, bursting
with wildflowers,
billowing clouds
against a cobalt blue sky,
the enchanting music
of birdsongs —
can be seen and heard.

In barely an instant,
the thick shroud of fog
returns with a dull thud —
the weight of it
no match for gravity,
and once again all is hidden
within its heaviness.

But those who were awake
for that one breathtaking
moment . . .
when the world was awash
in radiant light,
will ever know the place
in which they truly dwell.

Unconditional Love

It needs no reason for being —
neither is it earned nor authorized
in the giving.

It needs no doing —
merely intending —
its infinite tidal waves of radiant Light
ever ready to loose themselves
on a shadowed world.

It asks for nothing —
and bequeaths kingdoms.

I Felt the Goddess Rise

When at last I heard
the whispers,
the words of truth so
sweet and clear,
my soul said "Follow
the echoes," —
never mind that the path
they led me on
was a lonely one,
and there were no signposts
to guide me,
and the old familiar voices
were clamoring —
begging me to turn around,
warning me of the grave
dangers that lurked ahead.

But once I knew, I knew,
and there was no turning back,
so I whispered a prayer of thanks
for the precious gift I'd recently
been given —
the gift of awakening.

As I embarked on my soul's
long-fated journey,
the trance of unworthiness —
cast upon me at birth —
melted away like winter snow
in bright spring sunshine.

And I felt the Goddess rise.

Nudges from the Universe

Nights are filled with dreams of the Earth,
our precious home,
so desperately in need of our care,
and the great webbed circle of inter-being
that binds everything together —
plants and animals and people
and atmosphere and oceans.
I watch as a single strand
of the circle loosens and comes undone,
sending ripples coursing throughout the web,
loosening more tiny strands
that darken and dissolve.

A browning is underway.

The landscape abruptly shifts,
and once again I am a child,
awash in the remembered bliss
of lungs filled with the fragrant green air
that wafted through the woods of my youth,
and the loving kinship I knew
with every pine and maple and birch and oak.
The exquisite joy of playing among the trees!
How deeply my spirit was intertwined
with the spirit of the Earth!

A soft whisper floats across the dreamscape of my soul:
A great dying has begun —
        and this is the time you were born for.

I awaken,
knowing what it is I am being called upon to do.
I am overflowing with gratitude
for a patient, but persistent
Universe that nudges and prompts.
When we open ourselves to its wisdom,
it leads us into the fullness of our own being
until the path before us becomes clear,
and life's purpose shines with the brightness
of a thousand blazing stars.

To See Beyond

To see beyond an ancient window's foggy glass
and know the exuberant,
dancing brightness of summer's light,

to sink beneath the world's surface noise
and float in the warm, feathery softness
of life's great love song,

to glance in the mirror and see
a true reflection —
the resplendent essence of being,

to know deeper layers of reality
is to know that the Universe summons us
to awaken —
and come out to play.

Where Did You Take Me Last Night As I Dreamt?

Where did You take me
last night as I dreamt?
To what strange world
did we travel?

The moon was waltzing
across the midnight sky
with a dozen blazing comets
in its arms —
their shimmering tails
painting the heavens
in the most sublime light —
while the stars and planets
hummed a lovers' ballad
that deafened me to all
but honeyed murmurs
and soft strains of Love.

A mountain daintily
picked up her wildflower skirt
and tiptoed across the fields
to welcome me at dawn,
while the spirits of those
I have loved
greeted me joyfully
with a warm embrace
and words wrapped
in shimmering ribbons of Light.

How enchanting is a world
that trues the eye
and softens the tongue!
What place was this
that left me deaf to everything
but Love's music,
blind to all but
beauty and light and tenderness,
and able to speak only words
of loving-kindness?
What place was this?
Where did You take me last night as I dreamt?

Dreamers

Come, sit by my side
near the flickering fire.
We will drink steaming mugs of tea
and watch winter's brilliant sunset
and wonder aloud about this
world we find ourselves in.
Is it real? What is its essence?
Is it solid and ponderous and immovable
like a mountain?
Can we feel the weight of it in our hands?
Or is it fluid – like the fire's flame –
flickering and snapping,
creating shadows and light?
Is it form or formlessness – or both?
Are we part of a shared dream?

Oh, to tear apart this flimsy fabric
and slip outside to see what truly is!
Will we find a stage and scenery set in place –
arranged for us by an unseen hand?
Or, will we see only our reflections
at every turn –
the handiwork of our own creations?
Will we experience ourselves for the first time
and know our true essence?
Do we dare to dream a new dream?

It is so easily pierced, this fabric that binds us!
With but the tiniest of tears in its loosely woven fibers,
millions of possibilities rain down on us
like shooting stars
and scatter on the cold, sleeping earth around our feet.
How bright the glow of their potential!
How weightless our license
when we reap the dreams whose seeds
were sown in Love's infinite fields of light.

Sunrise

The coffee can wait,
the oatmeal will keep on the stove.
Let me extinguish the lanterns —
the morning has but this one sunrise.
I want to inhale its blazing fire
and lose myself in its rapture.

Jai Guru Deva.

Not Our Daughters

Let the call go out
to any and all
who would hear it —
to the grandmothers
and mothers and aunts,
and to the fathers
and grandfathers
and uncles and brothers —
to all who hold
love in their hearts
for our daughters
and granddaughters,
to all who have faith
in their goodness and judgment.

Let us rise as one
to answer the call,
knowing that these
are the days
we were born for,
these are the times we are
called upon to change.
Let us gather our
young women together
inside a fierce and powerful
circle of love —
an impenetrable circle
of protection —

formed from the light
that blazes brightly
in the hearts
of the women and men
who stand for them.

And to those
who would breach
the circle, we will say:
Know that there is
no force greater
than the force of our love
for our daughters.
We will not yield —
not today, not tomorrow.

May This Be Our Legacy

How far we have come from
the mystery and magic
we once knew.
The days and nights
of communal living,
the ceremonial circles
and celebration of seasons,
the healing wisdom
of the shamans
and mystical connections,
the synergies of survival.
Long forgotten are
our deep emotional
and spiritual connections
to the earth.

Yet somewhere,
buried deep within the core
of our collective being
lies a treasure trove of
truths tightly woven
into the fabric of our souls.
Everything we need
to transform ourselves and
the planet lies within,
if only we would remember.

Now is the time
to dream a new world into being—
healed, vibrant and beautiful.
A world we can be proud to
bequeath to our children
and grandchildren.

May we once again
become a tribal community —
an earth-wide tribal community —
aware of our connections
and interdependence,
evolving into a consciousness of unity.
May we walk more gently,
more intentionally,
upon the Earth,
filled with reverence
and gratitude —
for the world and
for each other

Let us sow the seeds
of love and healing today,
knowing we will not live to see
the full bounty of their yield —
but do so out of love for
the sons and daughters of the earth
who are yet to be.

May this be our blessing,
may this be our gift,
may this be our legacy
to the children
of tomorrow's world.

Forgiveness

Forgiveness bathed me
in its warm,
tender currents,
and carried me
high above the clouds.
Never more free was I.

Somewhere between the moon
and the beating heart
of the Universe,
the river of forgiveness
emptied into a sea
of unconditional Love —
and I came to know
the exquisite beauty of life.

The Way of Love

Anger and resentment settled in
like unwelcome house guests —
stubborn in their refusal to leave,
despite every effort to
ignore, cajole, and
sweep them away.
Still, they lingered,
unmoved by the chaos
they unleashed in my soul.
"The only way is the way of love,"
said my heart.

I thought of what I knew
of you,
the joys and sorrows —
the old deep pain rising like
a monolith from the depths of your being,
the still-smoldering wounds
inflicted just yesterday,
filling you with anguish and grief.
I felt the full weight of your suffering,
and stood on the edge of the inner abyss
you have kept so well hidden.
I realized I knew the abyss —
I too had spent many years
lost in its darkness.

But the light!
The blinding light of your
determined strength and bravery,
your steadfast refusal to succumb
to all that has harmed you!
How you strive to grow and change,
stubbornly setting your course
towards healing and love.

In the swirling brilliance of that light,
a gateway between worlds opened . . .
You were standing in the sacred breach,
and there was only the truth of who you are —
perfect, magnificent, aglow with
the incredible radiance of Spirit.

Having known your suffering
and the light of your strength and bravery,
having seen you as you truly are —
how could I not find forgiveness?
How could I not?
And how could I not love you?

At last, anger and resentment —
the unwelcome house guests —
disappeared from the landscape of my soul.
The empty space within
where destructive emotions had thrived
was inundated with powerful waves
of forgiveness and love,
and once again, my soul's dwelling place
was filled with the sweet, bright light of joy.

What is the Jingle of a Few Coins?

What is the jingle
of a few coins in a cloth purse
compared to the jewels of bliss
that lie within?

What is a gilded palace
glistening in the sun
compared to the light-filled
dwelling place of the soul,
where every tile
is fired in Love's blazing kiln?

How weightless are
our grievances and resentments
when measured against
the true fullness of being.

How like the soft flutter
of a butterfly's wing
against the skin
is our deepest pain,
once the exquisite joy
of the Self is made known.

How luminous is the world
when we awaken,
and see beyond the illusions.
How wondrous is the journey
when we discover
the riches lying within!

To Know

To know the tender Universal Force
that creates and dissolves patterns
and forms,

to know that we are of two worlds —
the boundaries between them
only imagined,

to know that the shape of the Universe is
a reflection of that which we dream
or otherwise summon,
and which unfolds
from within the realm of Spirit,

to know the fundamental unity that
connects us to each other
and to the All,

to know that this Earth school
demands much of us,
and we all lose our way
before finding it again,

to know that our every mistake
and wrongdoing contains
latent seeds of growth
that can lead us on the path
of spiritual evolution,

to know that we are never
judged by Spirit —
but always deeply loved,

to know that we are meant
to be here for one another —
to help and be helped,
to care and be cared for,
to love and be loved,
and to learn . . .

To know these things
is to know a much softer,
gentler Universe,
one in which there is no failure —
but endless growth and learning
and love.

Such is the true nature
of our shared journey.

Awakening

Showers of silky white light,
lustrous and glowing,
pour down from the stars
like a cloudburst on a sweltering summer evening,
drenching the moon,
swirling, glistening, painting
the world in silvery brilliance.
The light dances as it draws near . . .

An inner child bursts forth — unbidden —
leaving behind all that is burdensome,
running headlong into the sparkling deluge,
barefoot and laughing,
eyes wide in wonderment,
heedless of the reckoning!

i

Across the Years of Eternity

Have you ever watched a tiny gray cloud
gliding slowly beneath an ashen sky —
barely visible —
soft edges vanishing into nothingness,
wispy tufts breaking free, dissolving,
until the cloud disappears into
the infinite sky from which it came?

Afloat on currents of warm summer air,
thousands of microscopic water beads scatter —
until one day coming together again
to form a new cloud.

Are we the same —
minute little expressions
of something boundless, infinite —
forming, dissolving and re-forming
across the years of eternity?

The thought makes me smile.

Have You Heard The Sound of Daffodils?

Have you heard
the sound of daffodils
growing in the garden,
or smelled the sweet bouquet
of morning's sunrise?

Have you felt your soul
moving to the rhythms
of a dance troupe of trees
doing a tango in the wind,
or bathed in the cool fountains
of mist that rise
from the Earth at dawn?

Have you danced
to the melody of the spheres
as stars and planets
follow their courses
through the heavens?
Could you feel
the smooth flow
of cosmic order and harmony?

Have you known
the velvet rush of moonlight
flooding your veins,
or siphoned off
a drop of light
from the other realm —
and watched it become
a blazing star in the night sky?

Have you found yourself
in the company
of ancestors and spirits
on a quiet path in the woods —
and do they
fill your cup with love?

Have you known
moments of beauty and joy
so exquisite — so real —
that once experienced,
leave your heart forever
drenched in light?

How blissful and filled with wonder
is this journey through life
when we let our eyes adjust to the
Light of the Universe!

The Game of Love

In the rarely glimpsed realm
of the in-between —
that soft, warm space betwixt worlds,
where boundaries blur
or disappear altogether,
and light flows freely from one world to the next,
the playing fields,
where the game of love
is always underway,
are suffused with light.
In this realm of the in-between,
every bookmaker knows how to place his bets —
the odds are heavily weighted in favor of love.

Like a riotous group of fans wildly
cheering when their team
moves the score a point ahead,
all of creation rises, applauding,
raucously shouting its approval
when our score increases,
no matter that every rule is broken
along the way.
High jinks are presumed,
encouraged, even —
the outcome shamelessly rigged —
when the game is love.

Butterflies

A kaleidoscope of butterflies
float on currents
of sun-kissed air —
rainbows of iridescent hues,
swirling whirlpools of color, prisms
of blues and reds and yellows —
flowing forth from fluttering,
translucent wings,
transforming into
waves of Light
that rise and fall
with every delicate vibration
of their wings.

Dimming and brightening,
ebbing and flowing —
alive with the fiery radiance
of Creation
bursting into existence . . .
The eternal surges of Spirit's
life-giving imagination.

Trees!

Trees!
Verdant, vibrant and bright,
giddy with summer's gaiety,
dancing spirited dances
to the music of a passing breeze.
Like a well-practiced chorus line,
their high emerald skirts swish
to and fro —
sometimes as one,
sometimes like a wave rising here
and rolling across treetops to there —
leaving the forest awash in
June's wild green fragrance.
When summer fades,
they throw the earth a riotous party,
painting themselves in blazing costumes.

Barely concealed beneath summer's
brilliant greenery
and autumn's festive colors
and winter's powdery snow
and spring's burst of feathery new foliage,
a shining doorway to Elysium stands open —
ready to welcome all who find it.

A Tender Smile

To see a tender smile
is to watch the sky explode
into a kaleidoscope of
swirling colors —
glowing, radiant —
liquid light for a parched soul
to drink in.

When it is over,
its soft glow remains,
ever warming the heart,
ever brightening the world.

Stream of Light

How magical was the world
in the woods by the stream,
where a child could jump and splash
and hop across slippery, moss-covered rocks —
falling into the warm, shallow water —
echoes of her laughter filling the woods.

There was such joy
in endless summer days
of golden sunlight dancing
across bare arms and legs,
laying in the soft, warm sand
watching tadpoles swim,
sharing secrets with the trees,
finding small, sparkly stones —
diamonds and rubies and emeralds —
and sitting in the cool shade of the oak tree,
being gently lulled into a contented sleep.

Summers pass, children grow
and memories of enchanting worlds dissolve
into delicate threads that float away,
replaced by heavier, grownup concerns.
But always, some small, buried remnant
of unbridled joy remains . . .

Was it was inspired by a dream —
this longing to revisit a childhood sanctuary —
or was it a warm, insistent whisper rolling across
the landscape of her soul?
How her heart leapt in her chest
when she found the stream and the oak tree,
both of them shimmering and sparkling
in summer's dappled light.
After all this time, you're as perfect
and beautiful as ever,
she thought to herself, joy racing
through her veins.
"As are you," the oak tree whispered . . .

Would You Walk Through That Door?

What if the
doorway between worlds
has always stood open —
just inches in front of you —
and you could hear soft whispers
from the other side
inviting you to cross the threshold
and plumb the depths
of the Universe's wisdom and secrets?

What if your ancestors and spirit guides
have always offered you their
love and guidance?
If you became aware of their warm,
gentle encouragements,
would you pass through that doorway
to listen?

What if you knew that a carrying case
bearing your name awaited on the
other side of the door,
yours for the taking — no strings attached —
containing everything you might need
to succeed on this incredible journey
through life?
Would you step across the doorsill for it?

What if you need only
wipe the sleep from your eyes
and awaken to a different,
infinitely more joyful reality,
one in which you are always cherished –
as precious to the Universe
as a newborn baby –
watched over and guided
every moment of your life
with the most tender loving care?

What if you knew that the doorway
between worlds has always stood open –
for you?
Would you accept the loving gifts
the Universe offers you?
Would you walk through that door?

Bringers of Light

If we are to continue living on this planet,
we need to find a way out of the darkness,
find new ways of treating each other
and the Earth.
Destiny calls us —
every woman, young and old —
not with soft whispers
and gentle nudges,
but with powerful dreams
and calls to action
that tug on our souls and fill us
with pain and longing for a new world.
So we wipe away the thick,
odious fog of deception
that has clouded our vision
and kept us on our knees for centuries.
One by one, we reclaim our power,
and shatter — with swift precision —
the old ways that no longer serve us.
The old ideas and structures that imprison,
the words of war that divide and destroy
rather than unite and create...
With fierce, wild love that knows no bounds
and no exceptions,
and primal screams of joy
that explode into the cosmos,
we birth a new Earth into existence,
and a vibrant song of
hope, peace and oneness
is heard around the world.

We, the mothers and daughters and grandmothers,
we are the ones born to be the bringers of light,
the givers of unconditional love.
We are here, in this time and place,
to love away every last bit of hatred
and violence and intolerance in the world —
as only women can.
Destiny calls us.
We must answer the call . . . for the children.

www.ingramcontent.com/pod-product-compliance
Lightning Source LLC
Chambersburg PA
CBHW022041090426
42741CB00007B/1152